ALL RIGHTS RESERVED.
No portion of this book may be reproduced by any means whatsoever, except for brief quotations in reviews, without written permission from the publisher.

©Talk Too Much
Books 2018

You Don't Know Jack!

Quick, Easy, and Inexpensive Vegan Recipes Using Jackfruit!

Vegan on a budget Mini
Cookbook series

Table of Contents

Jackfruit Cooking Tips — Pg. 5
Jackfruit BBQ Ribs — Pg. 6
Jackfruit Buffalo Chicken Salad — Pg. 7
Jackfruit Crab Cakes — Pg. 8
Jackfruit Enchiladas — Pg. 9
Jackfruit Fried Chicken — Pg. 10
Jackfruit Loaded French Fries — Pg. 11
Jackfruit Nachos — Pg. 12
Jackfruit Pizza — Pg. 13
Jackfruit Pulled BBQ Sandwich — Pg. 14
Jackfruit Pot Pie — Pg. 15
Jackfruit Stuffed Potato — Pg. 16
Jackfruit Tacos — Pg. 17
Jackfruit Tuna — Pg. 18
Jackfruit Tuna Casserole — Pg. 19

Jackfruit Cooking Tips

1. Cook with canned jackfruit in water or brine. Canned jackfruit is picked young and therefore is not as sweet.
2. Always thoroughly rinse jackfruit to avoid tasting 'the can' or the distinct flavor jackfruit has.
3. The tough part of jackfruit can be discarded but those who prefer a grissle feel might want to consider using the tough triangular piece of jackfruit. It is edible.
4. Remove seeds before preparing jackfruit recipes. The seeds can be used to make hummus and other spreads.
5. Marinate jackfruit, whenever possible, to increase flavor absorption. Marinate for at least an hour or overnight in the refrigerator.

Jackfruit BBQ Ribs

Ingredients

1 can jackfruit
1 cup vital wheat gluten
1 tbsp. Smoked paprika
2 tbsp. Onion powder
1 tbsp. Garlic powder
1 tsp. Rib rub
½ cup vegetable broth
2 tbsp. Peanut butter
2 tsp. Liquid smoke
1 tbsp. Soy sauce
1 cup bbq sauce
Oil for frying

Directions

Preheat oven to 350°.
Lightly grease a baking dish.
In a medium bowl stir together vital wheat gluten, smoked paprika, onion powder, garlic powder & rib rub.
In a separate container, mix vegetable broth, peanut butter, liquid smoke, soy sauce. Whisk thoroughly.
Rinse and shred jackfruit. Add to wet mixture. Stir well.
Blend liquid ingredients with dry ingredients. Mix completely.
Knead for 2-3 minutes.
Spread and flatten mixture in baking dish.
Use a knife to outline ribs.
Bake for 25 minutes.
Remove from oven.
Warm oil in skillet. Fry ribs on both sides until charred to your liking making sure to baste with bbq as you fry.

Jackfruit Buffalo Chicken Salad

Ingredients

1 can jackfruit
⅓ cup buffalo sauce
½ tsp. Onion powder
½ tsp. Garlic powder
½ tsp. paprika
6 cups kale, spinach, or green leaf lettuce
1 large carrot, peeled and chopped
1 celery stalk, chopped
½ cup purple cabbage, thinly sliced
Salad dressing of your choice

Directions

Preheat oven to 350°.
Rinse, deseed, and shred jackfruit.
Warm oil in skillet.
Season jackfruit with all seasonings,
Cook jackfruit, over medium, heat for 5 minutes.
Add buffalo sauce. Simme for 10 minutes.
Transfer jackfruit mixture to baking dish.
Bake for 20 minutes until moisture is absorbed into jackfruit. Make certain to stir often.
Remove from heat and let cool.
Shred lettuce and top with carrots, cabbage, and jackfruit.
Top with dressing.
Enjoy!

Jackfruit Crab Cakes

Ingredients

1 can jackfruit
2 tsp. Ground flaxseed and 6 tbsp. Water, mix well and allow to sit for 10 min. (vegan egg)
1 tsp. Mustard powder plus 1 tsp. Water, mixed
2 tbsp. Old bay seasoning
1 tsp. Worcestershire sauce
½ tsp. Garlic powder
1 tsp. Lemon juice
¼ cup cilantro, finely chopped
2 Tbsp. fresh parsley, finely chopped
½ cup plain bread crumbs
½ cup panko bread crumbs

Directions

Thoroughly rinse and drain jackfruit
Chop jackfruit into tiny bite sized chunks
Mix everything, except the lemon juice, together and form into the patty size you desire
Refrigerate for an hour.
Preheat oven to 375° and put cakes on baking sheet
Squeeze lemon juice on top of crab cakes. Bake for 10 minutes.
Flip and bake another 10 minutes or until golden brown and firm

Jackfruit Enchiladas

Ingredients

2 cans jackfruit
1 cup vegetable broth
15 white corn tortillas
1 tsp. Onion powder
1 tsp. Garlic powder
½ tsp. turmeric
3 10 oz. cans enchilada sauce
2 cups shredded Daiya Cheddar
2 cups shredded Daiya Pepper Jack

Directions

Rinse. de-seed, and shred jackfruit.
Boil in vegetable broth for 5 minutes.
Season jackfruit with onion powder, garlic powder, and turmeric.
Mix chicken, ½ can of enchilada sauce, 1 cup cheddar and 1 cup pepper jack cheese.
Pour 1/2 can of enchilada sauce in bottom of baking dish.
Microwave tortillas until soft.
Roll divided chicken mixture into enchiladas.
Place rolled enchiladas into a baking dish.
Cover enchiladas with remaining 2 cans of enchilada sauce and cheese.
Bake at 350° for 25 minutes.

Jackfruit Fried Chicken

Ingredients

1 can jackfruit
1 ½ tsp. Smoked paprika
2 tsb. Dried basil
1 tsp. Dried dill
2 cloves garlic, minced
1½ tsp. Salt
1½ tsp. Pepper
1 tsp. Garlic powder
1 tsp. Onion powder
1 tsp. Turmeric
1 cup unsweetened almond milk
1 tsp. Apple cider vinegar
Vegetable oil for frying
1 cup chickpea flour

Directions

Combine milk, apple cider vinegar, ½ tsp smoked paprika, ½ tsp. Dried basil, ½ tsp. Salt, ½ tsp.
Pepper, Set aside.
Rinse and deseed jackfruit. Cut jackfruit into bite sized pieces. Add jackfruit to milk mixture and allow to marinate for at least an hour.
In a separate container, mix chickpea flour, and the remaining seasonings.
Warm oil in for frying until high temperature is reached.
Dip jackfruit into chickpea flour mixture coating pieces well.
Fry until golden brown.
Serve while warm.

Jackfruit Loaded French Fries

Ingredients

2 cans jackfruit, rinsed and drained
3 medium potatoes, peeled and chopped into fries
1 tsp. Olive oil
1 tsp. Smoked paprika
Salt and pepper to taste
½ sweet onion chopped
2 tbsp. Soy sauce
1 cup bbq sauce
1 tbsp. Arrowroot powder

Directions

Preheat oven to 425°.
In a bowl mix fries, oil, paprika, salt and pepper.
Mix well tossing until combined.
Spread fries on oiled baking sheet.
Place on baking sheet on top rack for 25 minutes tossing half way through.
Mix bbq sauce with arrowroot powder. Set aside.
Shred jackfruit.
Warm oil in skillet, add onion until translucent. Add shredded jackfruit and soy sauce until liquid
absorbs. Add bbq sauce. Mix well.
Transfer to baking dish.
Bake for 15 minutes at 400°.
Serve jackfruit on top of fries.
Serve while hot.

Jackfruit Nachos

Ingredients

1 can Jackfruit
½ cup salsa
4 cups tortilla chips
¼ cup chopped onion
¼ cup chopped tomatoes
¼ cup sliced jalapeno peppers
¼ cup sliced black olives
1 package Daiya Jack style block
1 8 oz bag Daiya cheddar style shreds
2 tbsp. Vegan margarine
½ cup unsweetened almond milk
1.5 tsp. Nutritional yeast
1 tsp. Oregano
1 tsp. Turmeric
2 tbsp. Taco seasoning
1 cup vegetable broth

Directions

Thoroughly rinse and drain jackfruit.
Chop jackfruit into bite size pieces.
Marinate jackfruit for at least an hour, overnight if possible.
Discard vegetable broth.
Season jackfruit with taco seasoning.
Fry jackfruit in olive oil over medium heat until lightly browned.

Cheese Sauce
Melt vegan margarine
Add the Daiya block and Daiya shreds, nutritional yeast, oregano, turmeric and milk.
Stir on medium-low heat for 5 minutes or until desired consistency is reached.
Layer tortillas with cheese, onions, tomatoes, jalapenos, olives, and salsa. Serve warm.

Jackfruit Pizza

Ingredients
Makes 1 Pizza

- 1 pkg. Daiya Mozzarella shreds
- 1 pk. Pre-made pizza dough
- 1 can pizza pasta sauce
- 1 ½ cup sliced mushrooms
- ¾ cup green pepper, chopped
- ½ cup basil leaves
- 1 whole green onion, thinly sliced
- 1 tbsp. Chili flakes
- 2 tbsp. Italian seasoning
- ½ cup olive oil
- 1 can young jackfruit
- 1 cup vegetable broth

Directions

Thoroughly rinse and drain jackfruit.
Chop jackfruit into bite size pieces.
Place vegetable broth and chopped jackfruit into ziploc bag. Marinate for at least an hour, overnight if possible.
Discard vegetable broth.
Season jackfruit with italian seasoning.
Fry jackfruit in olive oil over medium heat until lightly browned.
Spread sauce on top of pizza dough leaving about ½ inch from edge.
Spread cheese on top of pizza.
Top with mushrooms, onion, peppers and chili flakes.
Bake for 15-18 minutes at 400°.

Jackfruit Pulled BBQ Sandwich

Ingredients
2-3 Sandwiches

1 onion, chopped
2 cloves garlic, minced
2 cans young Jackfruit
Olive oil
½ tsp. Cumin
1 tsp. Liquid smoke
2 tsp. Smoked Paprika
2 tsp. Brown sugar
½ tsp. Red pepper flakes
¾ cup BBQ sauce
¼ cup Vegetable Broth
Salt and pepper to taste
Vegan ranch dressing
Buns
Lettuce
Tomato

Directions

Rinse, drain, and de-core jackfruit.
Shred jackfruit and thoroughly mix paprika, cumin, and brown sugar. Set aside.
Warm oil over medium heat Saute onion until translucent about 2-3 minutes adding garlic the last minute.
Add jackfruit. Cook for 3 minutes.
Add bbq sauce, liquid smoke, and vegetable broth and simmer another 15 minutes.
Build sandwich by placing jackfruit, tomatoes, lettuce and ranch on bun.
Serve warm

Jackfruit Pot Pie

Ingredients
2-3 Pot Pies

- 1 can jackfruit rinsed and de-cored
- 1 can vegan cream of mushroom soup
- 2 ½ cups unsweetened almond milk
- 2 cloves garlic or 1 tbsp. Garlic powder
- 2 bay leaves
- 2 sprigs of rosemary
- 1 tbsp. Olive oil
- 1 potato, diced into small chunks
- ⅓ cup carrots, cut into rings
- ½ cup frozen peas
- Puffed pastry

Directions

Heat olive oil in large pan over medium heat
Add jackfruit and onion. Fry 3-4 minutes.
Add garlic, bay leaves, rosemary, 1 cup almond milk and cream of soup.
Reduce heat and cover.
Simmer for 25 minutes.
Shred jackfruit and add remaining milk.
Add carrots, potatoes and peas.
Simmer another 20 minutes.
Remove bay leaves and sprigs.
Flour a work surface and roll out puffed pastry
Lightly grease baking dish. Cover dish with one sheet of puffed pastry.
Pour in jackfruit mixture.
Cover with remaining sheet of puffed pastry
Press sides with a fork. Brush top with butter.
Cut slits into pastry.
Bake in a preheated 375 degree oven for 15 minutes or until golden brown.

Jackfruit Stuffed Potatoes

Ingredients
Makes 4 potatoes

1 can jackfruit
1 onion diced
2 garlic cloves, minced
4-5 cremini mushrooms, sliced
½ cup vegetable broth
4 large baking potatoes
1 cup vegan sour cream
½ cup unsweetened almond milk
4 tbsp. Vegan butter
½ tsp. Salt
½ tsp. Pepper
1 cup vegan shredded cheese
8 green onions sliced

Directions

Preheat oven to 350°.
Bake potatoes for an hour.
Meanwhile….
Drain, rinse, and shred jackfruit. Set aside.
Heat oil in large skillet.
Add garlic and onion until translucent.
Add mushrooms and cook unt lightly browned.
Add jackfruit. Reduce heat and simmer for 15 min.
Add vegetable broth if jackfruit becomes dry.
Allow potatoes to cool.
Slice potatoes lengthwise.
Scoop out potatoes &
 place in bowl. Save the skin.
Add to potatoes sour cream, butter, milk, salt,
pepper, the jackfruit, ½ the cheese, and ½ the green onions. Mix well. Scoop mixture back in potato skins.
Top with remaining cheese and onions.
Bake for 15 minutes.

Jackfruit Tacos

Ingredients

Corn or flour tortillas
1 can jackfruit drained and rinsed
1 tbsp. Olive oil
1 small onion, finely sliced
2 cloves garlic, minced
1 tsp. Vegetable broth
1 tsp. Paprika
1 tsp. Chili powder
1 tbsp. Soy sauce
2 tbsp. Maple syrup
1 cup water
1 chipotle pepper in adobo sauce
Optional: lettuce, tomatoes, cheese, salsa, avocado, etc.

Directions

Shred jackfruit.
Marinate jackfruit in mixture of olive oil, paprika, chili powder, soy sauce, and maple syrup for at least an hour.
Heat oil over medium heat in frying pan.
Add onion, garlic, chipotle peppers and vegetable broth. Cook for 2-3 minutes.
Add jackfruit. Mix well and simmer for 30 minutes adding more vegetable broth if needed to prevent drying.

Build taco adding lettuce, tomatoes, cheese, or salsa

Jackfruit Tuna

Ingredients

1 can jackfruit
3 tbsp. Vegan mayo
1 tsp. Seaweed (use a seaweed sheet)
2 tbsp. Pickle relish
1 tsp. Old bay seasoning
1 tsp. Lemon juice
½ tsp. Himalayan salt
½ tsp. Black pepper

Directions

Thoroughly rinse and drain the jackfruit.
Shred the jackfruit. Season with old bay.
Bake jackfruit shreds in the oven for 30 minutes.
Allow to cool.
In a bowl, mix jackfruit shreds, mayo, seaweed (finely chopped), relish, lemon juice, salt and pepper.
Refrigerate for at least an hour.
Enjoy!

Jackfruit Tuna Casserole

Ingredients

1 can jackfruit
2 cups macaroni noodles
1 cup frozen peas, thawed
1 celery stalk chopped
1 garlic clove, minced
½ yellow onion, chopped
½ cup chopped mushrooms
3 tbsp. Nutritional yeast
2 cups unsweetened almond milk
½ cup vegetable broth
2 tbsp. Whole wheat flour
1 tsp. Onion powder
1 tsp. Garlic powder
½ tsp. Cayenne pepper
1 tsp. Old bay seasoning
½ cup bread crumbs
1 tbsp. Vegan butter

Directions

Preheat oven to 350°.
Cook macaroni according to directions.
Saute onion, garlic, and celery in olive oil.
Add mushrooms. Cook for 5-7 minutes.
Stir in milk and vegetable broth. Bring to a boil. Then reduce to a simmer.
Add nutritional yeast and flour. Allow to thicken.
Rinse, drain, and shred jackfruit.
Add jackfruit to milk mixture.
Poor macaroni and milk mixture into a baking dish.
Sprinkle bread crumbs on top.
Bake for 25-30 minutes.

Grocery List

1. _____
2. _____
3. _____
4. _____
5. _____
6. _____
7. _____
8. _____
9. _____
10. _____
11. _____
12. _____
13. _____
14. _____
15. _____
16. _____
17. _____
18. _____
19. _____
20. _____
21. _____
22. _____
23. _____
24. _____
25. _____

Grocery List

1. _____
2. _____
3. _____
4. _____
5. _____
6. _____
7. _____
8. _____
9. _____
10. _____
11. _____
12. _____
13. _____
14. _____
15. _____
16. _____
17. _____
18. _____
19. _____
20. _____
21. _____
22. _____
23. _____
24. _____
25. _____

Grocery List

1. _____
2. _____
3. _____
4. _____
5. _____
6. _____
7. _____
8. _____
9. _____
10. _____
11. _____
12. _____
13. _____
14. _____
15. _____
16. _____
17. _____
18. _____
19. _____
20. _____
21. _____
22. _____
23. _____
24. _____
25. _____

Grocery List

1. _____
2. _____
3. _____
4. _____
5. _____
6. _____
7. _____
8. _____
9. _____
10. _____
11. _____
12. _____
13. _____
14. _____
15. _____
16. _____
17. _____
18. _____
19. _____
20. _____
21. _____
22. _____
23. _____
24. _____
25. _____

Made in the USA
Columbia, SC
23 January 2024